And *Jackie Robinson*,
    a strong man,
    a fine man,
    whose courage in baseball
    brought equal rights
    for those of color.

    Whose Dodgers shirt
    hangs in ballparks today.

    The legacy of #42.

    It is the human spirit

    that we honor.

Baseball is the World Series

and *a championship team!*

Baseball Is...

LOUISE BORDEN

ILLUSTRATED BY RAÚL COLÓN

MARGARET K. McELDERRY BOOKS   New York   London   Toronto   Sydney   New Delhi

Baseball is our game . . .

the sport of America.

Its stories are stitched
through our nation's history.

Its teams and its heroes
we carry in our hearts.

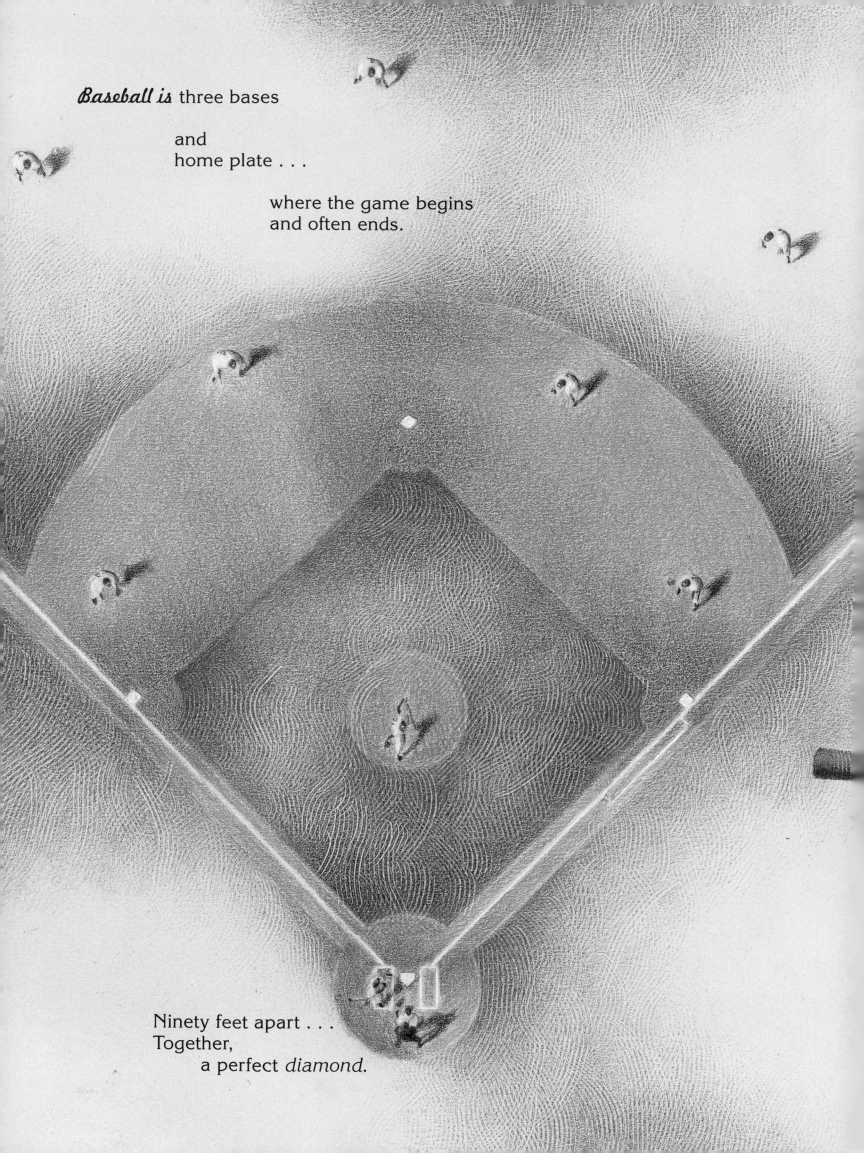

Baseball is three bases

and
home plate . . .

where the game begins
and often ends.

Ninety feet apart . . .
Together,
a perfect *diamond*.

And **baseball is** a ball that is pitched
and a bat that is swung
and gloves and rules

and *innings*.

And, of course,

baseball is *teams*
            and teamwork.

Baseball!

Such an exciting name
for our nation's game. . . .

Baseball is . . .

ballparks across America—
so very tall, so very grand—

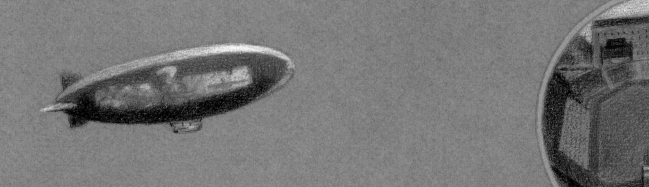

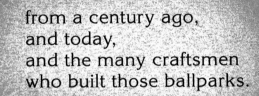

from a century ago,
and today,
and the many craftsmen
who built those ballparks.

Baseball is rivers of people

flowing across streets,

streaming onto ramps.

Baseball is wide gates to a swirl of noise,

ticket takers,

ticket stubs,

and vendors,

selling souvenirs.

Baseball is front row seats
and top row seats,
bleacher seats and box seats,

and always—always—
the buzz
of the spectators:

the fans.

And *baseball is* the field—

the field—
that expanse of beautiful green,

with a smooth swath of brown
between the infield

and the outfield.

Fences

    and foul poles

      and lines white with chalk . . .

      The snap of pennants
      in a summer breeze.

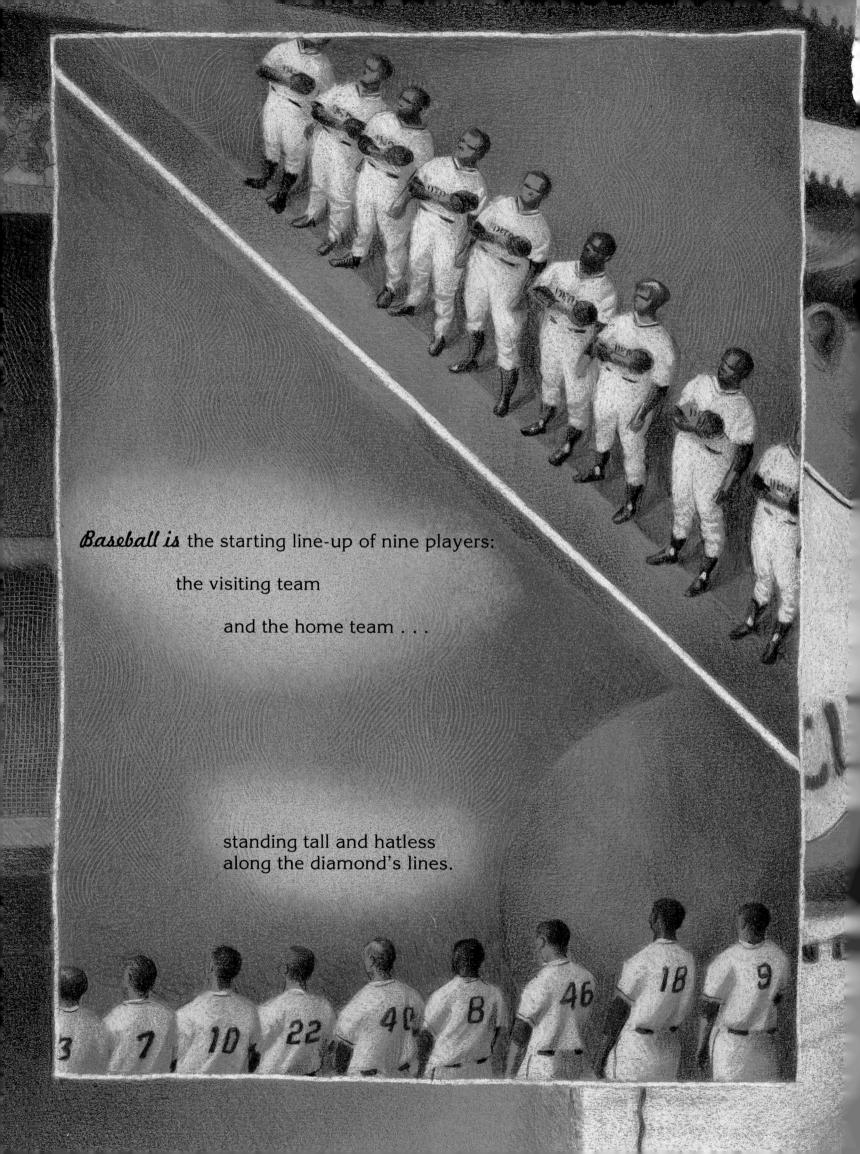

Baseball is the starting line-up of nine players:

the visiting team

and the home team . . .

standing tall and hatless
along the diamond's lines.

Baseball is . . .

America's anthem
before the game begins.

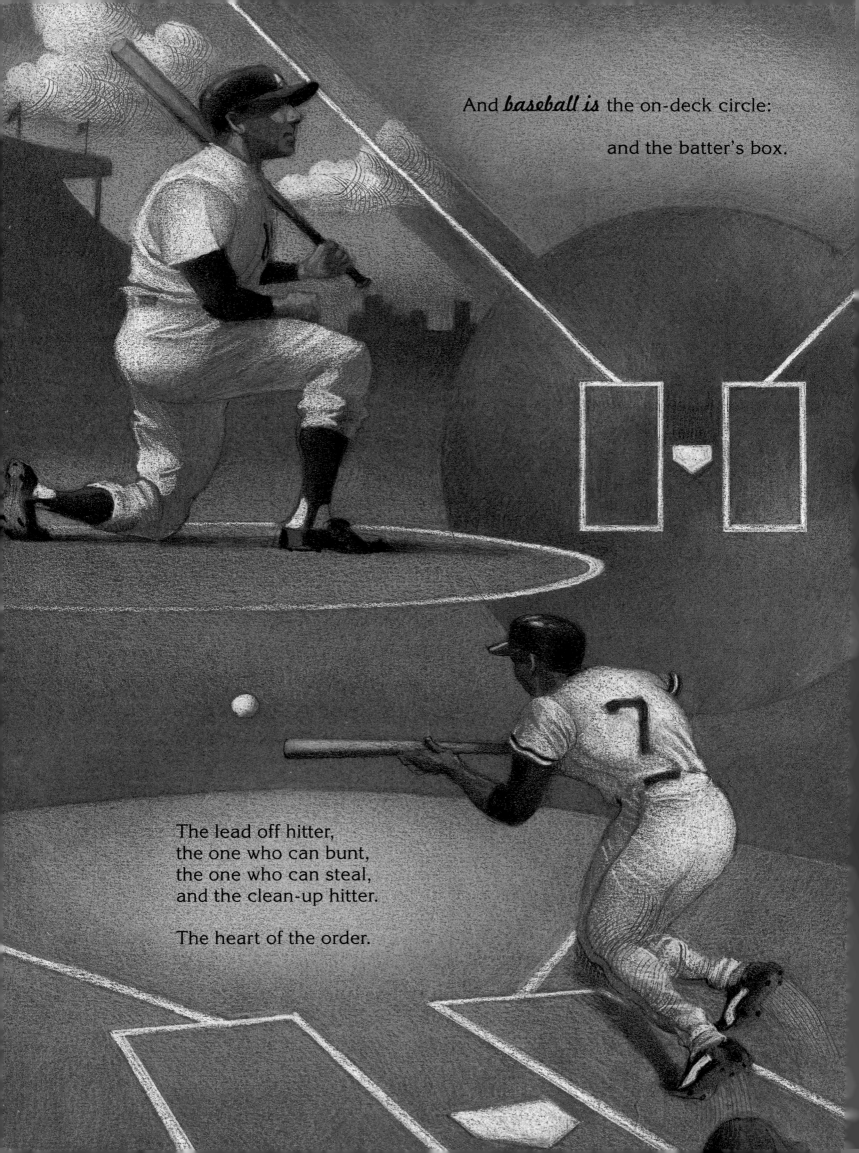

And *baseball is* the on-deck circle:

and the batter's box.

The lead off hitter,
the one who can bunt,
the one who can steal,
and the clean-up hitter.

The heart of the order.

And *baseball is* the rest of the team,

who sit in the dugout,
who lean against its railing,
who chew gum
or trade jokes,

who watch the action,
who hope and wait for *their* chance to play.

Baseball is the fastball,
the curveball,
the knuckleball,
the slider,

the crack of the bat,

the balk,
the steal,

the ground out,

the frozen rope,
the triple,

the squeeze play,
the double play,

the pop fly,
the sacrifice fly,
the warning track,

the walk, the RBI,

the error,

the tag,

and the *grand slam*.

Baseball is the scamper of the bat boy

and the distant shout in the stands:

"Peanuts!"

"Popcorn!"

Above the scene,
  like a familiar friend,

  red-and-white stripes,
  and fifty stars on a field of blue:

America's flag.

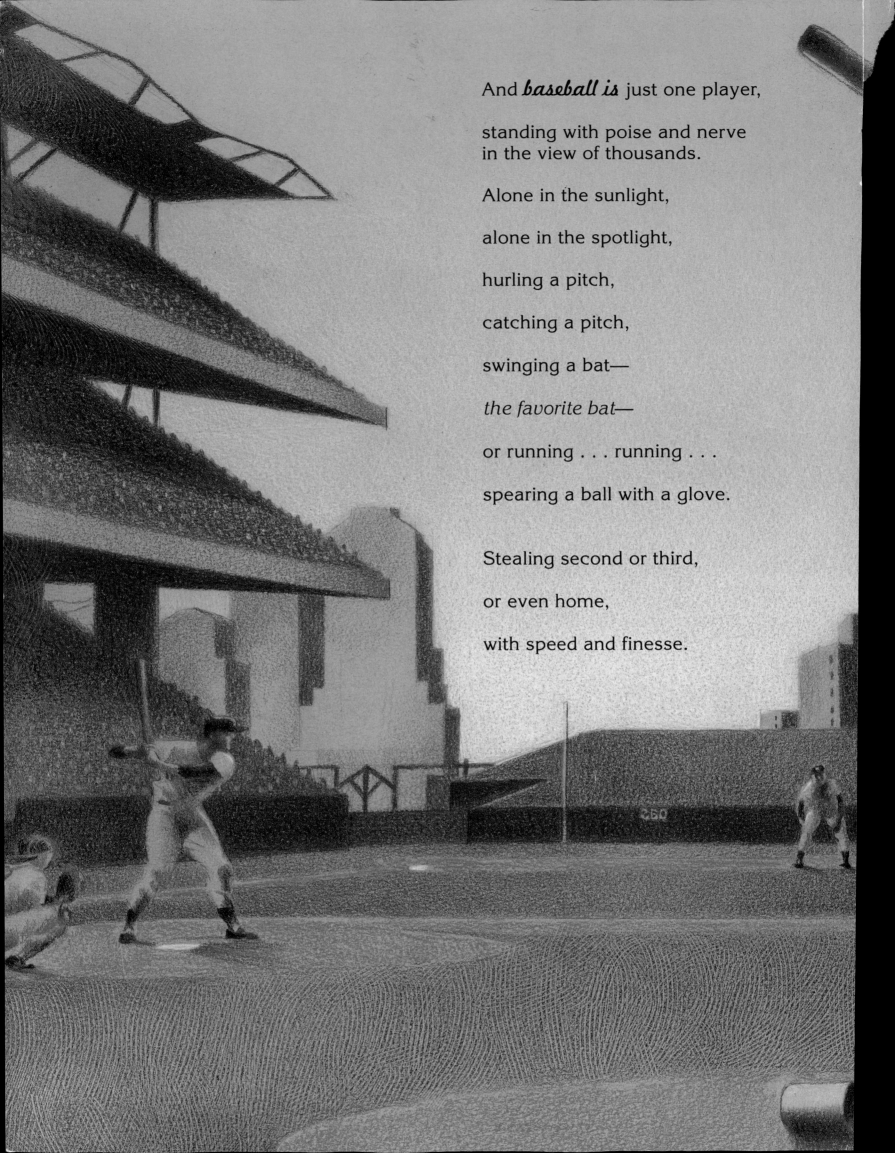

And ***baseball is*** just one player,

standing with poise and nerve
in the view of thousands.

Alone in the sunlight,

alone in the spotlight,

hurling a pitch,

catching a pitch,

swinging a bat—

the favorite bat—

or running . . . running . . .

spearing a ball with a glove.

Stealing second or third,

or even home,

with speed and finesse.

And *baseball is* any kid's glove,
carried from home to the game,

with hope,
with luck,

ready to catch a ball on the fly.

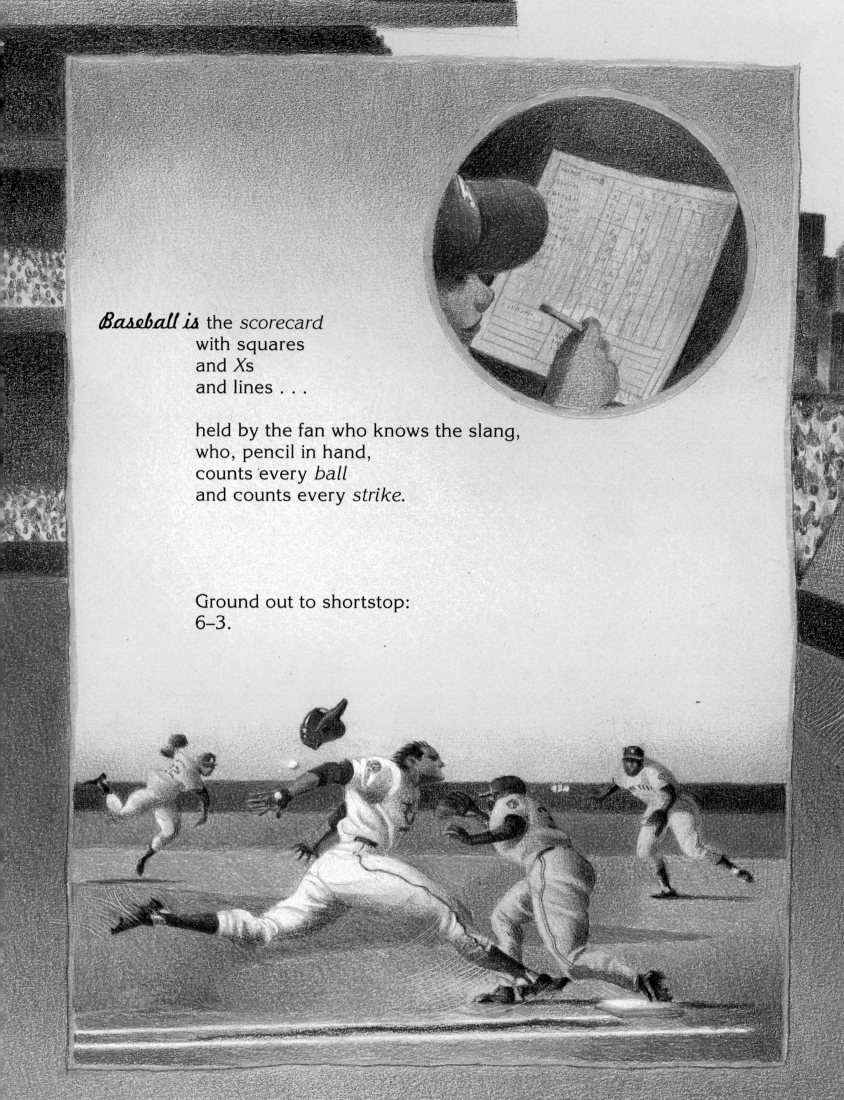

Baseball is the *scorecard*
with squares
and *X*s
and lines . . .

held by the fan who knows the slang,
who, pencil in hand,
counts every *ball*
and counts every *strike*.

Ground out to shortstop:
6–3.

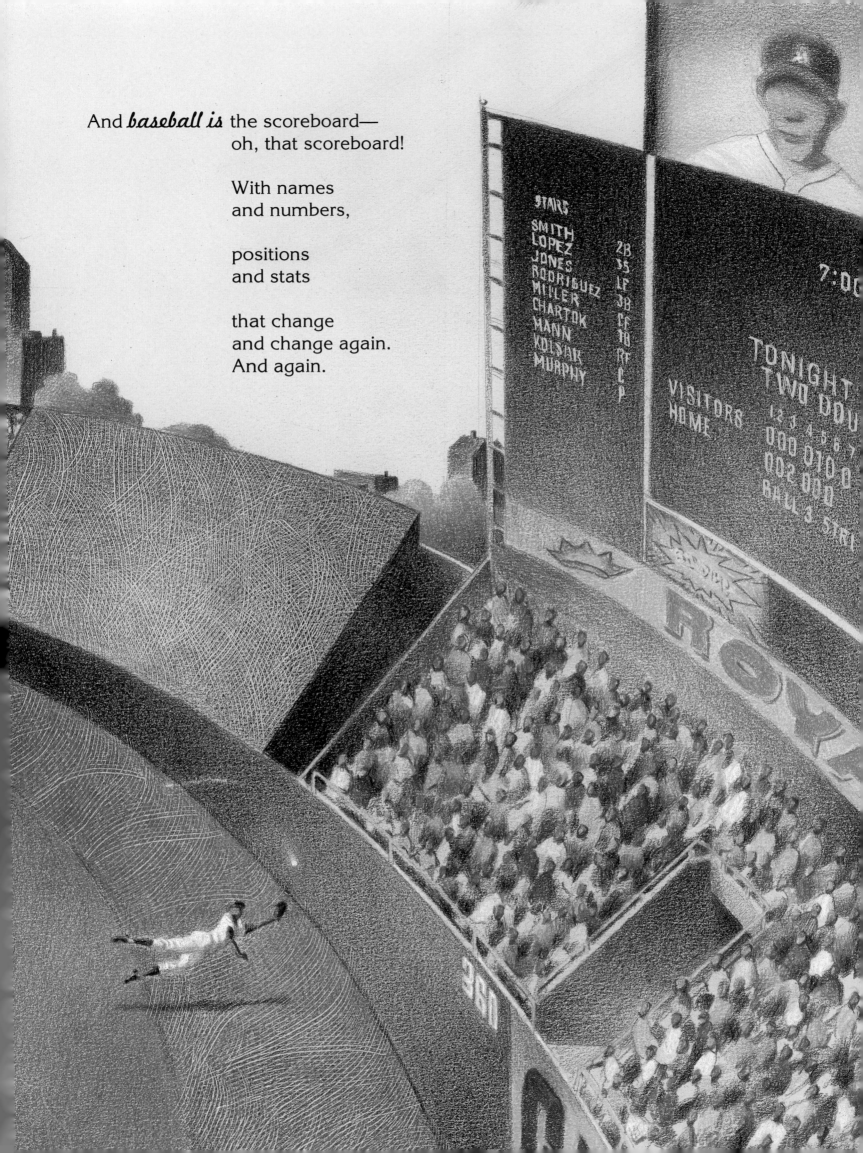

And *baseball is* the scoreboard—
  oh, that scoreboard!

  With names
  and numbers,

  positions
  and stats

  that change
  and change again.
  And again.

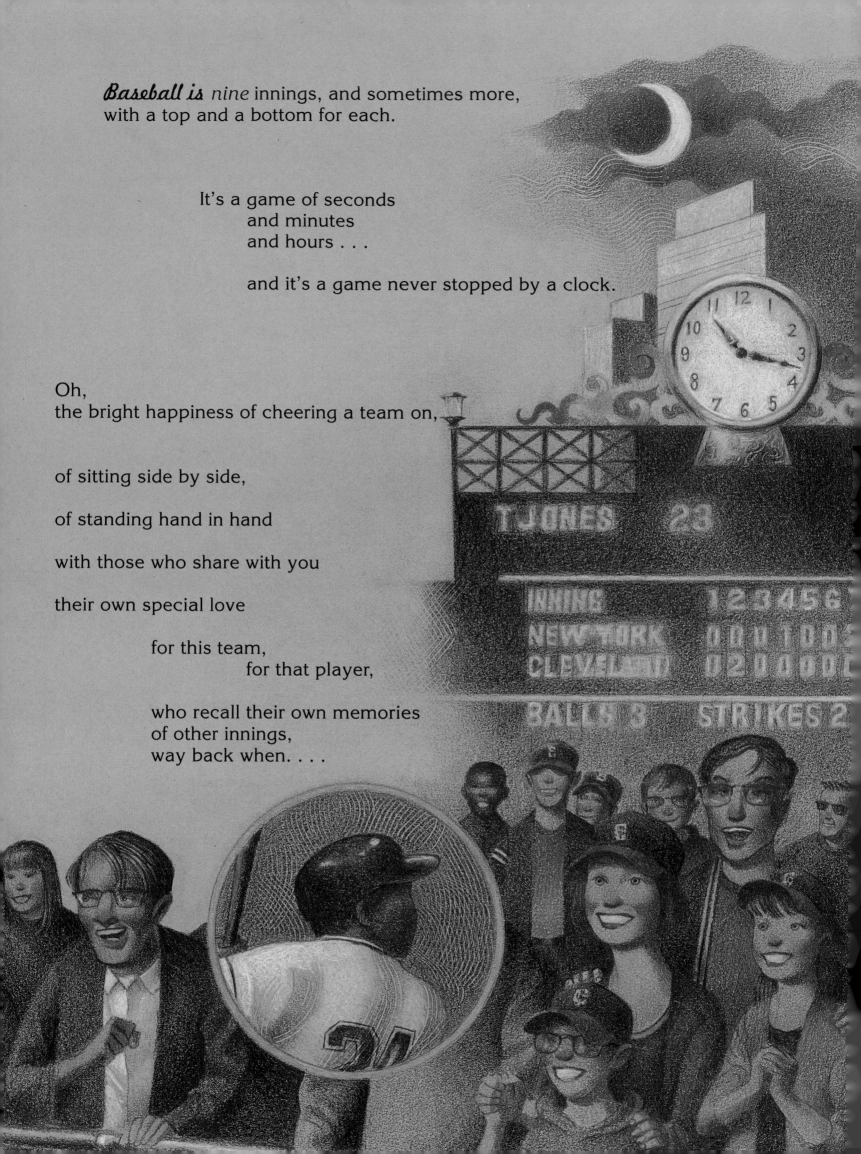

Baseball is nine innings, and sometimes more,
with a top and a bottom for each.

It's a game of seconds
and minutes
and hours . . .

and it's a game never stopped by a clock.

Oh,
the bright happiness of cheering a team on,

of sitting side by side,

of standing hand in hand

with those who share with you

their own special love

for this team,
for that player,

who recall their own memories
of other innings,
way back when. . . .

And *baseball is*

the seventh inning stretch,
when the fans belt out baseball's classic song:

"Take me out to the ball game. . . ."

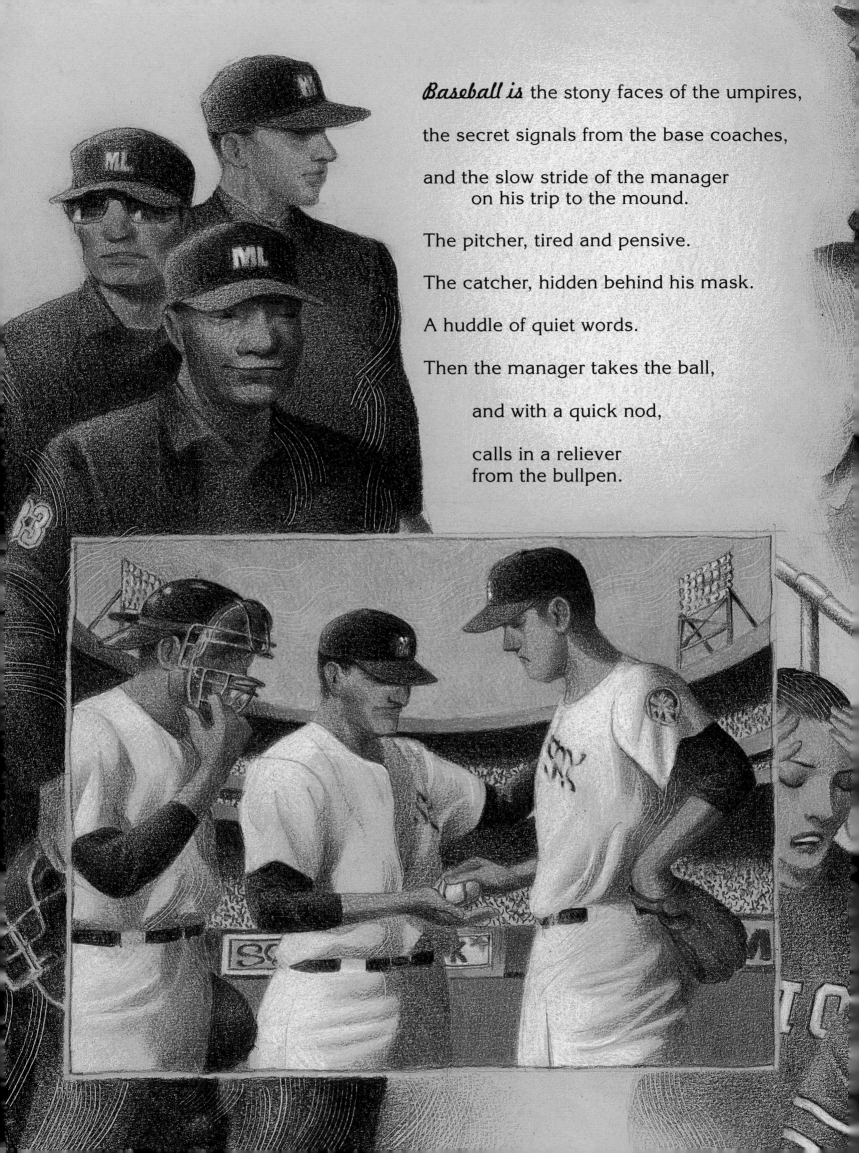

Baseball is the stony faces of the umpires,

the secret signals from the base coaches,

and the slow stride of the manager
on his trip to the mound.

The pitcher, tired and pensive.

The catcher, hidden behind his mask.

A huddle of quiet words.

Then the manager takes the ball,

and with a quick nod,

calls in a reliever
from the bullpen.

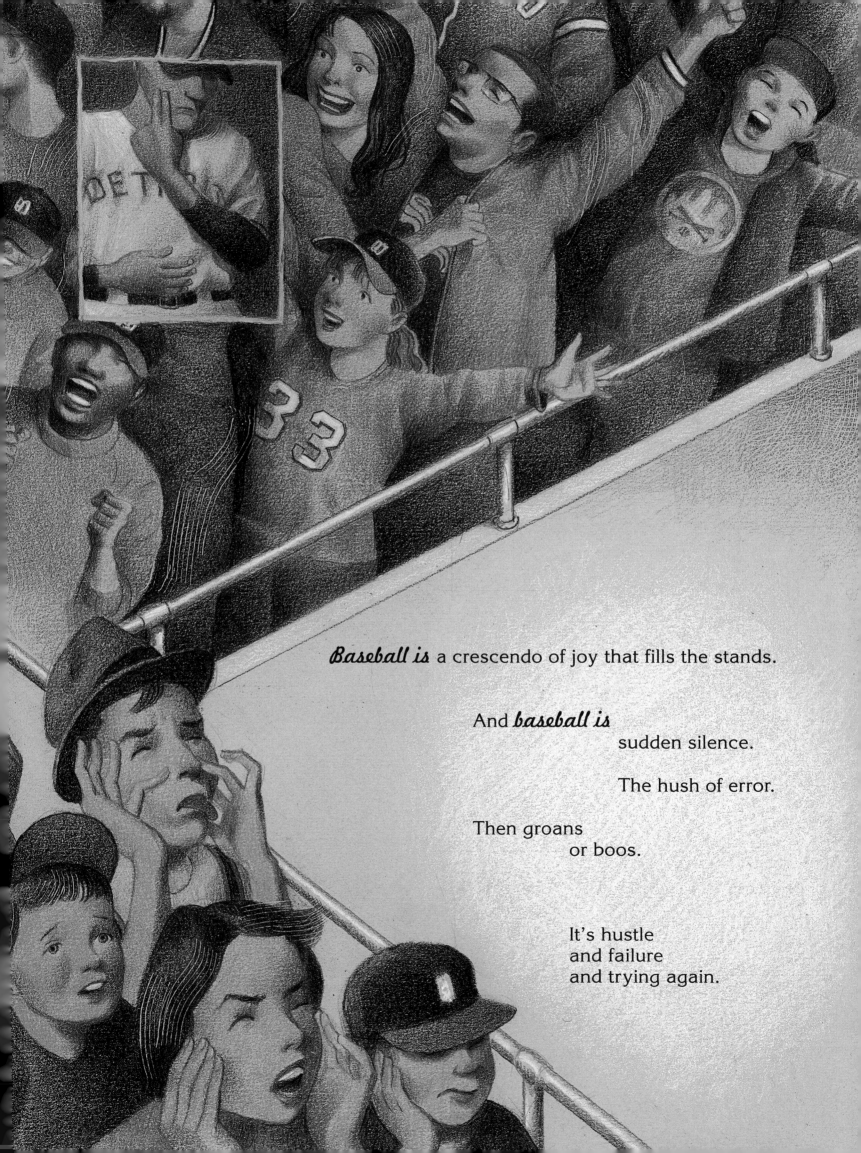

Baseball is a crescendo of joy that fills the stands.

And *baseball is*
sudden silence.

The hush of error.

Then groans
or boos.

It's hustle
and failure
and trying again.

Baseball is the announcers in the press box,

who know the stats of the day,

whose voices
bring us the sport's news
sent round the world on the Web;

who call the action
play by play;

and who remind us in the telling
that *this* game
is also *our* game.

The final score!

Two teams.
One winner.

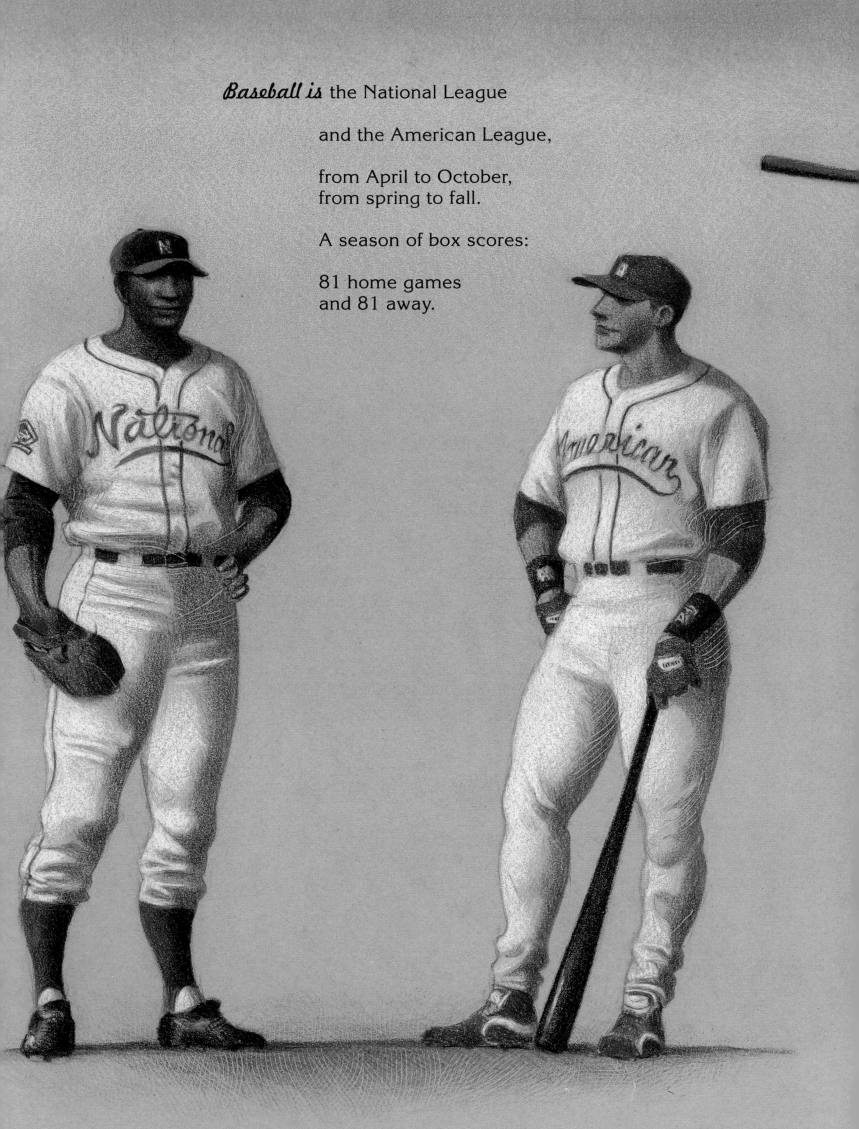

Baseball is the National League

and the American League,

from April to October,
from spring to fall.

A season of box scores:

81 home games
and 81 away.

And *baseball is* the minor leagues
and Little League,

the talented and long ago Negro Leagues,

the women's league,

and those thousands of *other* leagues and teams

from Maine to Michigan,
from Texas to Hawaii.

Baseball!

Baseball is razzle and dazzle,

rain and shine.

The All-Star Game in the middle of July.

And *presidents*,

yes, baseball is our *presidents*,

who join in our joy.

Baseball is razzle and dazzle,

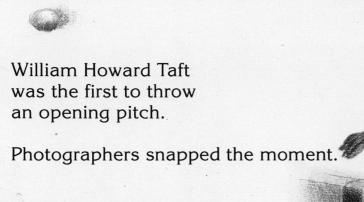

William Howard Taft
was the first to throw
an opening pitch.

Photographers snapped the moment.

FDR
pressed a telegraph key
to send a signal down the wires . . .
lighting Cincinnati's field
with a modern glow.
The first night game! Astonishing!

When our soldiers went off to war,
every team heard "Play ball!" . . .
to steady America's heart
in unsteady times.

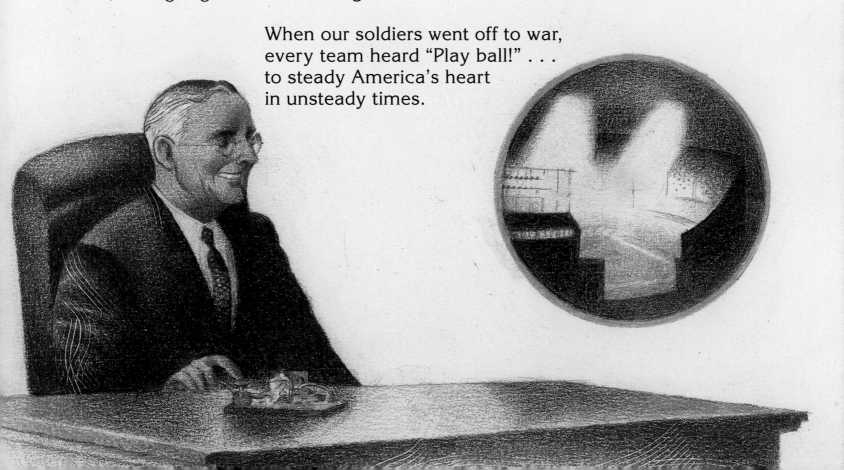

Baseball is a game of rookies and veterans.

Of nicknames.

Of style.

Baseball is Babe Ruth,

the greatest of the greats—

the boy from Baltimore's docks,
sent to a school for orphans
and toughs.

Who grew up to show the world
how to hit home runs.

Who penned his autograph
for thousands of young fans . . .

because for the Babe,
wherever he was playing,

it was the kids who mattered the most.

Like *Roberto Clemente*,
    the outfielder of speed,
    the humanitarian who showed Americans his skill,
    and the world,

    his dedication
    to those in need.

    And there are so many others
    who shine
    in baseball's hall of fame.

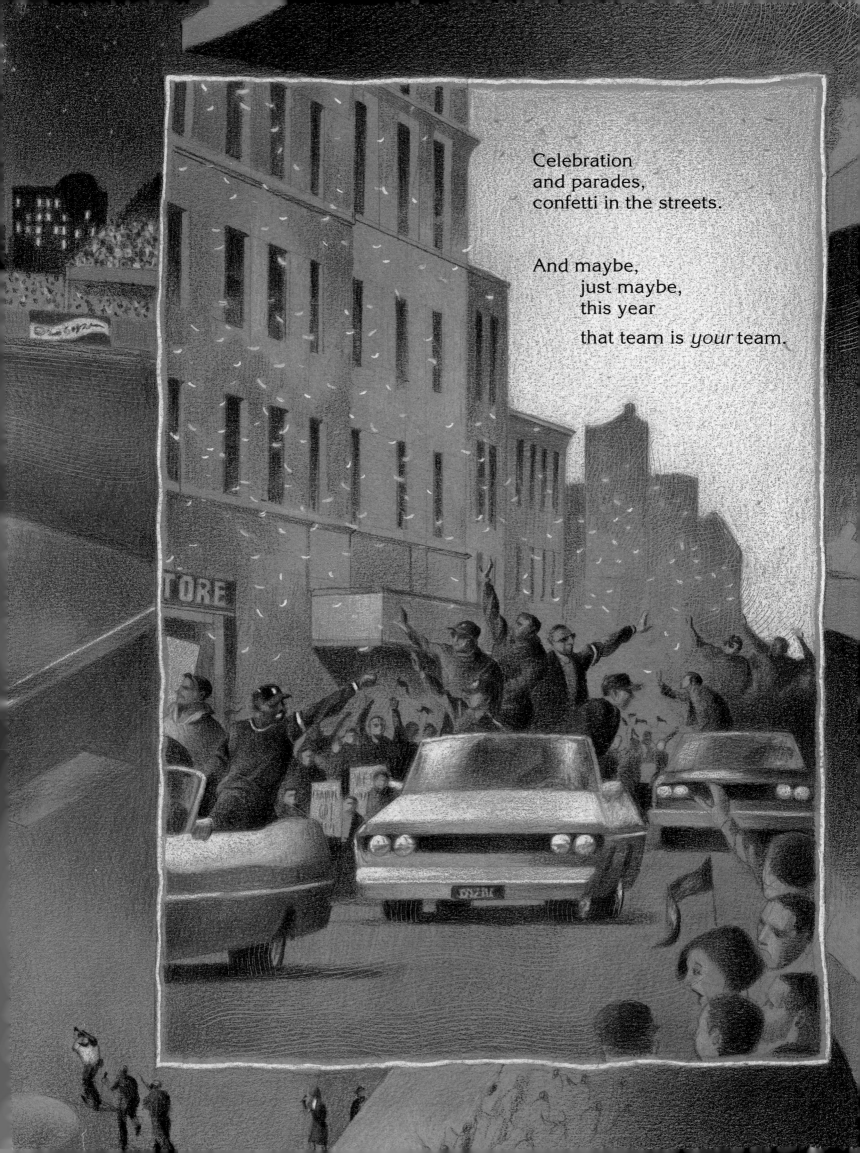

Celebration
and parades,
confetti in the streets.

And maybe,
    just maybe,
    this year

    that team is *your* team.

Because in baseball,

anything is possible.